SOCIAL LIVES:
ELEPHANTS

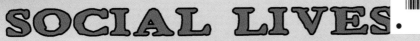

3 4028 09278 2458
HARRIS COUNTY PUBLIC LIBRARY

J 599.67 Sch
Schuh, Mari C.
Social lives of elephants
DISCARD
$8.95
ocn959225371

D1196749

ANIMAL BEHAVIORS

Mari Schuh

Rourke
Educational Media
rourkeeducationalmedia.com

Scan for Related Titles
and Teacher Resources

Before & After Reading Activities

Level: I

Teaching Focus:
Reading Comprehension: Use specific comprehension strategies, such as the use of story structure, to help students increase their reading comprehension.

Before Reading:

Building Academic Vocabulary and Background Knowledge
Before reading a book, it is important to set the stage for your child or student by using pre-reading strategies. This will help them develop their vocabulary, increase their reading comprehension, and make connections across the curriculum.
1. Read the title and look at the cover. *Let's make predictions about what this book will be about.*
2. Take a picture walk by talking about the pictures/photographs in the book. Implant the vocabulary as you take the picture walk. Be sure to talk about the text features such as headings, Table of Contents, glossary, bolded words, captions, charts/diagrams, and Index.
3. Have students read the first page of text with you then have students read the remaining text.
4. Strategy Talk – use to assist students while reading.
   - Get your mouth ready
   - Look at the picture
   - Think…does it make sense
   - Think…does it look right
   - Think…does it sound right
   - Chunk it – by looking for a part you know
5. Read it again.
6. After reading the book complete the activities below.

Content Area Vocabulary
Use glossary words in a sentence.

charge
emotions
examine
grieve
mammals
reunite

After Reading:

Comprehension and Extension Activity
After reading the book, work on the following questions with your child or students in order to check their level of reading comprehension and content mastery.
1. *Why do baby elephants stay in the center of a herd?* (Summarize)
2. *What is a group of elephants called?* (Asking questions)
3. *What do elephants do when a member of their herd dies?* (Text to self connection)
4. *After reading the book, what can you summarize about elephants?* (Summarize)

Extension Activity
Elephants use their trunks to not only smell but to feel things. Fill a box with many different objects. Now it's your turn to be the elephant! Have your friends or classmates put socks on their hands and then reach into the box and try to guess what they are feeling with their "trunk."

Table of Contents

Social, Emotional Elephants

Elephants live together in groups called herds. These giant **mammals** form strong friendships.

Elephants also form relationships with people and other animals such as rhinos.

Elephants are social creatures. Their behaviors may express their **emotions**, or feelings, to other elephants.

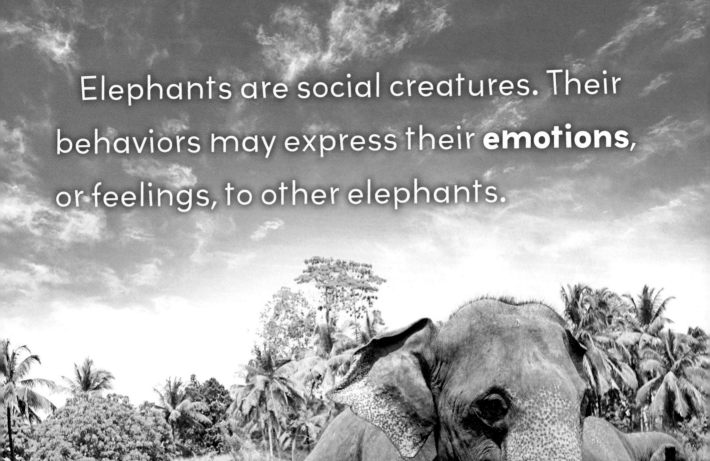

Elephants can show kindness. A hurt elephant might walk slowly. The herd waits for the slow elephant to catch up.

Elephants help each other. A young elephant might get stuck in mud. Other elephants help it get out. Sometimes elephants also help people who are hurt.

Elephants seem to love their young. They hug them with their trunks. They watch out for their young and keep them close by.

Young elephants stay in the center of the herd. They are surrounded by older elephants and kept away from danger.

Fear and Grief

Elephants might feel anger or fear when they sense danger. They roar. Their ears and trunks are alert.

An older female elephant leads and protects the herd. She will **charge** toward a dangerous animal to keep the herd safe.

Elephants may **grieve** and feel sadness. They cry and scream when other elephants die. Their trunks hang down. The elephants walk slowly and have less energy.

Elephants often stay with a dead elephant for days. They are quiet while they stand by the body.

Elephants seem to bury their dead.
They put leaves, branches, and soil on the
dead body.

Elephants **examine** the bones of dead elephants. They gently touch and smell them. Sometimes they pick up the bones and carry them away.

Elephants are smart animals. They might be able to tell if an elephant's bones belong to an elephant they knew.

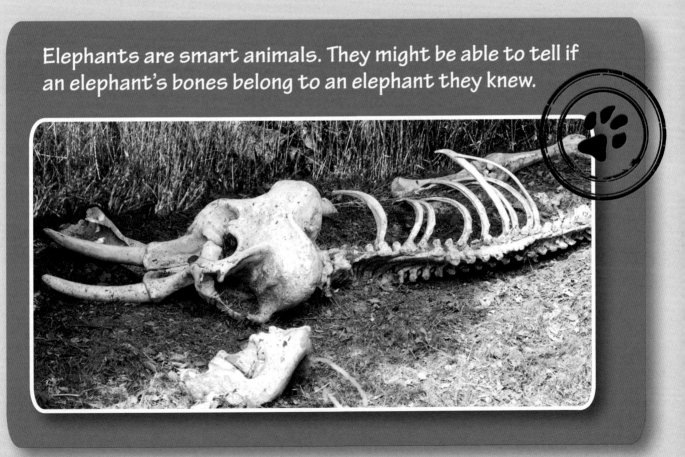

Sharing Joy

Elephants may feel joy. They seem happy when a calf is born.

Many females gather near the newborn calf. The excited group waves their trunks. They make trumpet-like sounds.

Fluid can flow from an elephant's eyes. This could mean the elephant is feeling a strong emotion.

Elephants also seem happy when they play. They chase each other and kick their legs in the air.

They wrestle and climb on each other.
They play in mud and wiggle on the
ground.

Sometimes elephants do not see each other for a long time. The elephants show joy when they **reunite**. They make rumbling sounds as they rush to be together.

The elephants roar loudly as they flap their ears. Some elephants spin in circles. The elephants are excited and happy. They are together again.

Elephants have great memories. They can remember people and elephants they knew many years ago.

Photo Glossary

charge (charj): When animals charge, they rush at people or other animals in order to attack them.

emotions (i-MOH-shuhnz): Emotions are strong feelings. Joy, love, and grief are emotions.

examine (eg-ZAM-uhn): When people and animals examine something, they inspect it and carefully look at it.

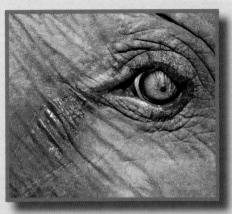

grieve (greev): When people and some animals grieve, they are very sad, usually because someone has died.

mammals (MAM-uhls): Mammals are animals that are warm-blooded, have hair or fur, and feed milk to their young.

reunite (ree-you-NITE): To reunite is to be together after being apart for a long time.

Harris County Public Library
Houston, Texas

Meet The Author!
www.meetREMauthors.com

Websites to Visit

www.discoverykids.com

www.kids.nationalgeographic.com

http://kids.sandiegozoo.org

About the Author

Mari Schuh is the author of more than 200 nonfiction books for beginning readers, including many animal books. She enjoys a quiet life in Wisconsin with her husband and their lazy house rabbit, Kindle. You can learn more at her website: www.marischuh.com.

Library of Congress PCN Data

Social Lives of Elephants / Mari Schuh
(Animal Behaviors)
ISBN 978-1-68191-704-7 (hard cover)
ISBN 978-1-68191-805-1 (soft cover)
ISBN 978-1-68191-902-7 (e-Book)
Library of Congress Control Number: 2016932583

Rourke Educational Media
Printed in the United States of America, North Mankato, Minnesota

© 2017 Rourke Educational Media

All rights reserved. No part of this book may be reproduced or utilized in any form or by any means, electronic or mechanical including photo-copying, recording, or by any information storage and retrieval system without permission in writing from the publisher.

www.rourkeeducationalmedia.com

PHOTO CREDITS: Cover © Johan Swanepoel; Page 5 © SurangaSL; Page 6 © Graeme Shannon, Page 7 © john michael evan potter; Page 8 © mariait, Page 9 © Four Oaks; Page 10 © Ronsmith, Page 11 © JONATHAN PLEDGER; Page 12-13 © john michael evan potter; Page 14 © Artush, Page 15 © Svetlana Foote; Page 16 © JONATHAN PLEDGER, Page 17 © vicspacewalker; Page 18 © topten22photo, Page 19 © Albie Venter; Page 20 © Johan Swanepoel, Page 21 © Steve Lagreca; Page 22 (top picture). All images from Shutterstock.com

Edited by: Keli Sipperley
Cover design, interior design and art direction: Nicola Stratford
www.nicolastratford.com

Also Available as: